Scrapbooking Made Easy

Designer Die Cuts

To my friends Scarlett and Holly:
Here's to stormy nights and die cut art.

Jill A. Rinner

introduction

One of the most fun and economical ways of adding color and shape to your layouts is with die cuts. When they are embellished, they look even better (hey, who doesn't?)! But what happens if you don't have access to a die cut machine to cut endless shapes? Or if the store you shop at doesn't carry all the shapes in various colors for layering, now what? What if you're just cheap (um, I mean economical) and don't want to have to buy the same shape in five different colors just to make it look interesting?

In this book, I will show you some fabulous tricks to turn your plain, ordinary die cuts into designer die cuts! You will learn the many techniques of die cut art and the secrets to get you on the path to designing die cuts on your own. In no time, you'll have fabulous die cuts to enhance any layout!

die cut couture

I have always loved the word "designer." Most of America has too, seen by the way we have snatched up designer labels over the years. It lends an air of mystery, a fashion secret that is waiting to be discovered along the cat walks of Paris. Well, this isn't exactly Europe, and there isn't any flowing fabric to drape over a waifish body (yes, that totally describes me), but there is paper! And we have die cuts! And, by golly, we want to make them designer, right? Well, Ralph Lauren was busy, so you're stuck with me. But that's not half bad because I know die cut secrets I want to share with you and he doesn't!

First things first, every designer needs some tools. The good news is, as a scrapbooker, you probably have all of these, and the better news is that you get to put them to use again! Here's what's needed:

GLUE PEN—a chisel tip glue pen is great for all those delicate areas you need to glue when working with die cuts. I also use a broad tip one as well. A glue stick will also work.

SMALL SCISSORS—all the precision trimming needed for this art will be much easier to handle with a short-blade (sharp tip) pair of scissors.

RULER—make sure there are not any nicks in the side of your ruler if it is plastic. They break the flow of the pen and make the finishing work look sloppy.

METALLIC OR OPAQUE MARKERS—these are a die cut designer's best friend. Black in various tips is a must have too. I couldn't live without my fine-point silver, gold and white opaque pens!

CRAFT KNIFE AND CUTTING MAT—these are for the fine precision cutting sometimes needed while embellishing your die cuts.

PERSONAL TRIMMER—straight, crisp lines are a must with designing die cuts, and a personal trimmer will cut your paper exactly where you want.

EMBOSSING STYLUS AND LIGHT BOX—these will be your new secret weapon with a technique I've created that helps you create a fabulous layered look.

ADDITIONAL DESIGNING TOOLS—these are punches in various sizes and shapes and a paper crimper to help add that extra flair to your die cuts.

I know you are anxious to jump right in and start designing fabulous die cuts, but there are a few guidelines to remember. Die cuts have a wrong side and right side to them. When looking at the right side of the die cut, the edges will be turning downward to create a finished-edge look. Make sure the right side is showing before starting to add embellishments to your die cut.

When trimming off excess paper from layers you have added, always turn the die cut over to the wrong side so you can see the original shape of the die cut and then trim off the excess paper. This will keep your die cut in its perfect original shape and will give you professional results when using the many design techniques.

DESIGNER DIE CUT DICTIONARY

double duty (dub´ əl d o͞o´ tee) n. **1.** when two die cuts of the same shape but different color are placed together to create dimension (see GRASS) **2.** when two die cuts of different shapes but with common themes are put together to create a paper representation of a realistic object (see JAR OF JELLYBEANS and BATHTUB AND MAT). *Each die cut may be embellished with a marking pen, simple layering or other technique before combining into a duo.*

The samples shown here are to get your creative juices flowing. Look around and notice the items in your surroundings. Think of how these things would look if they were a die cut and needed to be embellished. What would you use? What different colors or textures would you add? Keep the design techniques in mind as you observe your world and find inspiration to embellish your die cuts.

simple layering (sim´pəl lā´er -ing) *n.* **1.** when a single die cut is enhanced by adding other pieces of cardstock in various methods. **2.** adhering cut stripes (see TIE), letters (see PENNANT) or shapes (see BARN) on top of the die cut. **3.** placing different colors behind the die cut to show contrast through the images in the shape (see LADYBUG). **4.** mounting the die cut onto contrasting cardstock and carefully tracing around the pattern with scissors to create a mat effect (see SUN). **5.** replacing simple shapes of the die cut with various colors using scissors or a personal trimmer (see TRAFFIC LIGHT). **6.** using a part of another color die cut in the same shape that may be too difficult to recreate on your own (see BLOW DRYER). *Glue should always be applied to the original die cut on the wrong side [back], so it will not seep through from the added piece to the finished side.*

Look at stickers for color and shape ideas for layering your die cuts. Mrs. Grossman™ brand stickers are my favorite to look at for inspiration in embellishing my die cuts. The colors and lines used are so crisp and distinctive and will inspire you many times over.

advanced layering (ad vanst´ lā´er -ing) *n.* **1.** layering contrasting pieces on top of a die cut to enhance its dimension with the use of a stylus and a light box to create the shaped piece (see footnote for further explanation). Generally this technique would require having the same die cut in several different colors so it can be cut apart and layered. Sometimes this is not convenient. *Original die cut should remain intact and not be trimmed off, thereby creating a base to build layers on.*

Footnote: Place original die cut on a light table or bright window right side up, so you can see through the perforated lines that create dimension on the die cut. Place a scrap of cardstock in the desired color directly on top of the area you wish to layer. Using an embossing stylus, rub the tip of stylus along the outline of the area you wish to create a contrasting color for, pressing lightly into the paper. Remove paper from die cut and you should see the outline of the shape you need to layer your die cut. Use your scissors to carefully cut along the line created by the stylus. Place finished piece onto your die cut and glue into place.

making lines (māk -ing linz) *n.* **1.** using marking pens to add dimension and personality to die cuts (see BLOCKS and CAR). **2.** using marking pens to outline die cut design for added detail (see FLOWER). **3.** using marker lines to add additional color on die cut that needs to be visually softer than layering paper (see BACON). *Photo journaling can also be added to the die cut with markers. Opaque markers work best for this design technique (refer to recommended supplies).*

Organize your die cuts by subject, so they can easily be found when you are working on beach pages or holiday pages (refer to the booklet on organizing).

adding punches (ad -ing punch´ez) *n.* **1.** using punches to add additional designs to die cuts to make them cuter (see BALLOON and SNAKE). **2.** using punches to enhance original marking on a die cut (see OCTOPUS). **3.** using punches to change the look of one original die cut and make it into a small work of paper art (see FLOWER POT and TREE). **4.** using a circle hole punch to create polka dots on any die cut. Instead of gluing dots onto die cut, original die cut is punched out creating the holes directly in it, then a contrasting color in the form of a scrap paper or additional die cut is placed behind the first die cut allowing the color to show through holes for a polka dot effect (see FISH and STRAWBERRY).

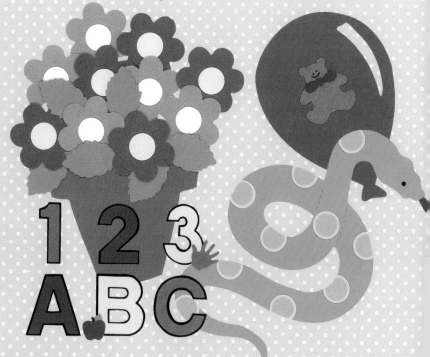

By changing the color of a die cut from what you might normally expect, you can alter the whole effect of what it can be. For example, a horse, which is normally found in browns, can be made in black or white to create a zebra with contrasting stripes. Blocks can be made in pastel colors for baby blocks, primary colors for children's building blocks and white for ice cubes!

adding stickers (ad -ing stik´ərz) *n.* **1.** placing sticker designs on top of die cut to add more color and design to the original shape. **2.** before creating total look, sticker is placed very lightly on die cut to determine placement and how well it will look. Once it is pleasing to the eye, smooth down firmly into place. *If any portion of the sticker is hanging off the die cut and the adhesive back is exposed, rub baby powder on the back to neutralize the adhesive (dust works very well for this purpose and is much handier, simply run finger along available furniture and rub collected dust on the back of the sticker for the same effect!).*

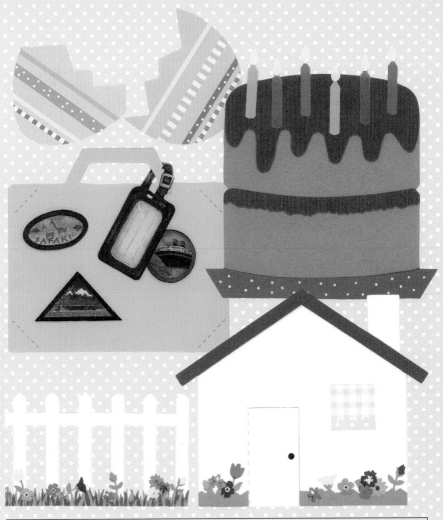

Think outside the box with your die cuts. For example, the popcorn that comes with the box can be made into a Christmas garland with berries added or used as pollution clouds coming out of the back of a car.

scissor power (siz´ ər pou´ ər) *n.* **1.** cutting a creative edge into a die cut for visual interest (see CRAB). **2.** layering a die cut with a contrasting color and trimming with a creative-edge scissors to add texture (see STARFISH and SAND DOLLAR). **3.** creating interesting design lines to add pizzazz to a die cut (see SOMBRERO). **4.** adding punches for a 3-D effect and trimming them with creative-edge scissors before layering on a die cut (see TRUCK). *Keep scale in mind. Scissors with a smaller pattern work best with die cuts.*

Save all those paper scraps and organize them by color so you can find what you need without having to rummage through a huge pile. I keep mine in expandable pocket files that are color coded to what's inside.

fancy paper (fan´sē pā´pər) *n.* **1.** using metallic paper to enhance elements of a die cut that would have shiny surfaces on the realistic item (see SUNGLASSES and CAMERA). **2.** using pattern paper to make the die cuts cuter and more interesting to look at (see CHAIR and CRAYONS).

Coloring books are great places to find distinct shape references. If you look at a picture of a car, notice all the shapes and colors that make it look dimensional. Incorporate those into your die cuts with the help of pens and/or punches.

paper crimping (paˊpər krimp -ing) *n.* **1.** using a paper crimper to create texture and movement on a die cut. Die cut can be placed in crimper diagonally to create motion (see WAVE). **2.** die cut may be folded before crimping to make cool effects of texture (see TREE). **3.** a portion of the die cut may be cut off and then crimped (see CUPCAKE and PENCIL). **4.** a die cut can be crimped in one direction and then reinserted in the crimper going the other direction to create a waffle effect (see ICE-CREAM CONE). **5.** two separate die cuts may be crimped and then layered together (see SUN). *To reduce bulk added to your scrapbook, after crimping pull the design apart slightly. This will not eliminate the effect of crimping.*

What makes a "basic" come alive? Designers will tell you it's the finishing touches—the added flair that makes it something unique. Add that something special to your die cuts and let them be the finishing touch that brings personality to those basic layouts.

About the Author

Jill Rinner is a nationally recognized authority on scrapbooking. She has taught hundreds of classes about the many facets of scrapbooking—from the basics to advanced, creative lettering and much more. Jill is a frequent contributor to *Creating Keepsakes*™ magazine.

Photo taken in Cape Cod, MA.

When she is not scrapbooking, Jill loves to spend time with her husband and their three children. She also enjoys gardening, traveling, organizing and reading. Jill lives in Okemos, Michigan, where she is the co-owner of a fabulous scrapbook store called Our Favorite Things.